The Boy Who Fell

Born in London in 1939, Alan Ayckbourn spent most of his
childhood in Sussex and was educated at Haileybury.
Leaving there one Friday at the age of seventeen, he went
into the theatre the following Monday and has been working in it ever since as, variously, a stage manager, sound
technician, scene painter, prop-maker, actor, writer and
director. These last two talents he developed thanks to his
mentor, Stephen Joseph, whom he first met in 1958 upon
joining his newly formed Studio Theatre Company in
Scarborough. A BBC Radio Drama Producer from 1965 to
1970, upon the early death of Stephen Joseph he returned
to Scarborough to become the company's Artistic Director.
He holds the post to this day, though the theatre is now
named after its founder. He is the author of over fifty plays,
most of which received their first performance at this
Yorkshire theatre, where he spends the greater part of the
year directing other people's work. More than half of his
plays have subsequently been produced in the West End,
at the Royal National Theatre or at the RSC. They have
been translated into over thirty languages, are seen on
stage and television throughout the world, and have
received many national and international awards. Alan
Ayckbourn was appointed a CBE in 1987, and in 1997
became the first playwright to be knighted since Terence
Rattigan.

ALAN AYCKBOURN

The Boy Who Fell
into a Book

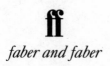

faber and faber

First published in 2000
by Faber and Faber Limited
Bloomsbury House
74–77 Great Russell Street
London WC1B 3DA

Typeset by Faber and Faber Ltd
Printed and bound by CPI Group (UK) Ltd, Croydon, CR0 4YY

A CIP record for this book
is available from the British Library

ISBN 978-0-571-20334-5

The Boy Who Fell into a Book was first performed at the Stephen Joseph Theatre, Scarborough, on 3 December 1999. The cast was as follows:

Kevin Charlie Hayes
Rockfist Slim Richard Derrington
Voice of Dad, Gareth, Rumpelstiltskin, Ebenezer, Daddy Woobly Julian Forsyth
Brunt, Bishop, Wolf, Narrator, Headless Monk Robert Austin
Monique, Mummy Woobly Nicola Sloane
Pawn, Queen, Little Red Riding Hood, Jennet, Baby Woobly Dorothy Atkinson

Director Alan Ayckbourn
Designer Roger Glossop
Lighting Mick Hughes
Costumes Christine Wall
Music John Pattison

CHARACTERS

Kevin, a boy of ten
Rockfist Slim, a fictional detective

At Kevin's house:
Voice of Dad

In *Rockfist Slim and the Case of the Green Shark*:
Monique
Brunt, her henchman

In *Chess for Beginners*:
A White Pawn
A Red Bishop
Gareth, a Red Knight
The White Queen

In *Grimm's Fairy Tales*:
Rumpelstiltskin
The Grandmother/Wolf
Little Red Riding Hood

In *Kidnapped*:
Jennet
Ebenezer

In *The Wooblies' Picnic*:
Voice of the Narrator
Daddy Woobly
Mummy Woobly
Baby Woobly

In *The Book of Ghost Stories*:
The Headless Monk

Actor 1 Brunt, Bishop, Wolf, Narrator, Headless Monk

Actor 2 Dad, Gareth, Rumpelstiltskin, Ebenezer, Daddy Woobly

Actress 1 Monique, Mummy Woobly

Actress 2 Pawn, Queen, Little Red Riding Hood, Jennet, Baby Woobly

ACT ONE

Kevin's bedroom.
  Kevin is in bed, reading aloud.

Kevin '. . . Rockfist Slim, ace detective, fought like a crazed tiger. Whap! One evil-looking, scar-faced opponent crashed to the ground, floored by a powerful Rockfist special. Thwang! Doinng! Another thug reeled back, thudding against the wire-mesh screen. Ooof! Thunk! Boof! A knife-wielding heavy ran headlong into the concrete wall as Rockfist stepped nimbly aside. Aaaargggh! A fourth flew helplessly through the air, victim to our hero's well-oiled combat skills. Aaarrggh! Uuurrg! Grroof! Soon the old warehouse was strewn with the groaning bodies of defeated opponents who had learnt the hard way not to tangle with Rockfist Slim. But still they kept coming. It appeared that the underworld leader known only as the Green Shark was this time taking no chances. Eventually, sheer weight of numbers bore Rockfist to the ground. Semi-conscious but still struggling, Rockfist was dragged across the concrete floor. He was dimly aware of a heavy iron door screeching open. The next moment he was thrust inside one of the disused smelting ovens.

The door clanged behind him. Rockfist found himself in deep, impenetrable darkness . . .'

Dad (*off, calling*) Kevin!

Kevin (*calling*) Dad!

Dad Is your light still on?

Kevin (*switching his bedside light off immediately*) No, Dad.

Dad It had better not be. It's half past ten, son.
Now, go to sleep. I've told you before, if you want
to read, read in the daytime.

Kevin Yes, Dad.

Dad Goodnight then, son.

Kevin Goodnight, Dad. (*He waits a few seconds,
listening. When he thinks the coast is clear, he
reaches out and switches on the light again.*)

Dad (*immediately*) Kevin!

   Kevin switches off the light swiftly.

I won't tell you again!

Kevin I was just – looking for the light switch,
Dad.

Dad Go to sleep.

   *Pause. Kevin puts the book away on his bedside
shelf alongside five others.*

Kevin How can I go to sleep in the middle of a story? I can't go to sleep till I know what happens to Rockfist. He could be dying. He's trapped in an oven. There mightn't be enough air in there. He could suffocate. Or maybe they'll light the oven. Then he'd be roasted to death. (*He ponders.*) Or they could flood it with water, or gas or . . . any-thing . . . The trouble is . . . with a book, it's not like a film . . . with a book . . . a good book . . . it's up here, inside your head . . . and you're like . . . inside the book . . . it becomes . . . part of you . . . real . . . really real . . . really . . . really . . . really . . . real . . . (*He falls asleep. He tumbles forward. His bed disappears. He wakes up with a cry.*) Wah! (*He looks around him. He is in a small pool of light. Everywhere else is in darkness. He gets to his feet.*) Where am I? What is this place?

Voice (*from the darkness*) Hold it right there, kid.

Kevin (*jumping*) Who's that?

Voice I said, don't move. I've got a .22 in my sock, a .38 in my vest and a .45 pointing straight at you, so don't move a whisker, kid, or you're target prac-tice.

Kevin Who are you?

Voice Put up your hands and throw down your gun.

Kevin I can't do that.

3

Voice Do as you're told or you're dead puffin.

Kevin It's an impossibility. How can I put up my hands and then throw down my gun? It's physically impossible.

Voice (*after a slight pause*) OK, then. Throw down your gun, then put up your hands.

Kevin I can't do that either.

Voice (*angrily*) Now listen, kid, this ain't negotiable . . .

Kevin I can't. I haven't got a gun. (*He holds out his arms. He is clearly unarmed.*)

Voice Who are you? What are you doing here?

Kevin My name is Kevin Carter and this is my bedroom.

Voice Your *bedroom*? This is your bedroom?

Kevin Yes.

Voice What are you? Some kind of weird hermit?

Kevin (*suddenly doubtful*) At least, I think it's my bedroom. It was a minute ago. Anyway, I might ask you the same thing. Who are you and what are you doing here?

> *A cigarette lighter clicks in the darkness. The room fills with light, revealing Rockfist in snap brim trilby and trenchcoat.*

Rock The name's Rockfist Slim, kid.

Kevin Rockfist –? You're Rockfist –? You're Rockfist Slim? *Rockfist Slim?*

Rock (*impatiently*) Yeah, Rockfist Slim. Rockfist Slim, OK? Who the hell are you?

Kevin I've told you, I'm Kev –

Rock Yeah, Kerry Carthorse, OK. But what are you doing –?

Kevin Carter. Kevin Carter.

Rock Yeah, OK. So what are you doing here?

Kevin I was – I just . . . (*looking around*) What is this place –?

Rock You don't know?

Kevin No.

Rock I thought it was your bedroom.

Kevin I – well, it isn't any more. It's . . . Where are we?

Rock We're in what we term in my line, kid, a tight spot. A place they only let you out of feet first. Generally they leave you to die.

Kevin (*in wonder*) It's the old smelting oven . . .

Rock Believe me, it'll smell even worse in an hour.

Kevin You've been shut in here by the Green

Shark's men, haven't you?

Rock Green Shark? What do you know about the Green Shark?

Kevin Quite a bit.

Rock (*menacingly*) You working for the Green Shark?

Kevin No! I'm just . . . I'm . . .

Rock How do you know about the Green Shark?

Kevin I'm – I'm reading the book.

Rock Book? The Green Shark's brought out a book?

Kevin No – it's – hard to explain. I –

Rock Listen. Just level with me, huh, kid? What are you doing here?

Kevin I was – You're not going to believe this . . .

Rock Try me. I'll believe you. If you tell me the truth, I'll believe you.

Kevin (*rapidly*) I was in bed reading a book called *Rockfist Slim and the Case of the Green Shark* and I was halfway through it when my dad told me to turn out the light or he'd get cross, and so I turned out the light and I was sitting there in the dark, thinking about the story, and then suddenly I was falling, falling and the next minute I ended up here.

Rock I don't believe you.

Kevin Told you, you wouldn't.

Rock Whoever you are, you shouldn't be here. You may be crazy but you shouldn't be here.

Kevin I know I shouldn't. I just seem to have – fallen in.

Rock OK. So fall out.

Kevin I can't. I don't know how to. I don't know how I get home.

Rock Listen. I'd like to help you. But I can't keep you around. I've got problems of my own. I'm locked in here, there's no way out and I have less than seventy-two hours before the Green Shark destroys half the planet. All you've got to do is get home. I'm trying to save the world here, kid.

Kevin I know.

Rock You know?

Kevin I'm halfway through the book. It's very serious.

Rock You bet it's – Book? Listen, what's with the book?

Kevin It's – Well, you see. You're in a book.

Rock I'm in a book.

Kevin Yes. This is a book. We're both in a book.

Rock We're both in a book.

Kevin Right.

Rock Are we both in the same book, by any chance?

Kevin At the moment. I think we are.

Rock I don't think we are. I don't even think we're on the same planet. Less than seventy-two hours to go and I'm trapped in an oven with a lunatic kid. What am I doing here? I don't even like kids. I hate kids. Get out of my oven. Get off my planet. Let me out of here.

Kevin Listen. I'll do a deal with you.

Rock A deal? What kind of deal?

Kevin If you – if you help me to get home – I'll help you solve your case.

Rock Oh yeah?

Kevin How about it?

Rock How do you plan to do that?

Kevin Because back home I have – your book. If I got home I could – find out what happens.

Rock How do you do that?

Kevin I'd skip on ahead.

Rock Skip on ahead?

Kevin How about it?

Rock Kid, would that life was that simple. We'd all be skippin' on ahead, believe me.

Kevin I could. I could do it.

Rock You could do that?

Kevin Easily. Trust me. Please.

Rock Don't get me wrong, I'm used to being in books. I been in thirty-four books thus far. But generally when they get around to writing the book it's after I've solved the case. What you're propositioning here is that someone's got in ahead of me. Like God or the IRS. Still. Anything's worth a try. Given this posthumous information at your disposal, could you find out the identity of the Green Shark?

Kevin I'm sure I could.

Rock If I knew his identity I could stop him. But he moves like he's invisible. You can never see him. He could be anyone. He could be a she. He could be a dog. He could be you. (*staring at Kevin*) No, he couldn't be you.

Kevin Why not?

Rock Because the Shark's intelligent –

Kevin I'm intelligent –

Rock If you're so intelligent what are you doing trapped in an oven with me? Come on, let's find a way out of here . . .

Kevin Listen, if I help you, you have to help me . . .

Rock Maybe.

Kevin Is it a deal?

Rock (*reluctantly*) It's a deal.

They shake hands.

OK. Now stand back.

Kevin What are you doing?

Rock I'm going to charge that door. (*He strikes his lighter again, briefly.*)

Kevin It's made of iron.

Rock So am I, kid. Stand back. (*He rushes at the door, vanishing into the darkness. There is a dull clang and silence. In a moment he returns, limping and clutching his shoulder.*) Let's start looking for another way out.

He begins to start exploring in other directions. Kevin stands still, thoughtfully.

Kevin A smelting oven. Now . . . Let's think . . .

Rock You going to help me or just stand there talking to yourself?

Kevin Just a minute. Can I borrow that lighter of yours?

Rock What do you plan to do? Burn the place down?

Kevin Please.

Rock Here.

Kevin Thanks. (*He strikes the lighter. The room is brightly lit again.*) It's bright.

Rock It's been recently refilled.

Kevin (*looking upwards*) Yes. Look, there is.

Rock What?

Kevin Up there. A chimney. This is an oven. So there has to be a chimney.

Rock (*gazing upwards with him*) I was just about to say the very same. You any plans about how to get up there?

Kevin If you give me a hand, I'll have a go.

Rock OK. It's your neck.

Kevin Not if I fall on you.

Rock (*as Kevin returns his lighter*) No problem. I'm made of steel, kid. (*He winces, the lighter's hot. Making a step with his hands*) Put your foot there.

Kevin (*doing so*) Right!

Rock And hup!

Kevin clambers up on to Rockfist's shoulders and grasps the edge of the chimney opening.

Hey! Hey! Hey! Steady, there . . .

Kevin (*as he struggles*) I thought you were – made of – steel . . .

Rock Make that tin plate . . . ow . . .

Kevin (*triumphantly*) Done it! I'll start climbing.

Rock Hey! What about me?

Kevin I'll be back.

Rock (*to himself*) Now he's left me here. (*consulting his watch*) Sixty-nine hours and we'll all be dead and he leaves me here to die . . . (*calling*) Hey, kid, where you gone?

Kevin (*reappearing*) Here. (*He drops a rope down to Rockfist.*) Can you climb that?

Rock (*testing it cautiously*) Possibly. I was a marine for a short period.

Kevin Come on, then.

Rock What's this tied to?

Kevin The chimney stack.

Rock Does it look safe?

Kevin Fairly safe.

Rock Terrific.

He climbs up and together they reach the open air. They stand regaining their breath.

Hey. Some view from up here.

Kevin Yes.

Rock Beautiful night.

Kevin Certainly is, after that oven.

Rock You see up there? That's Fido, the dog star.

Kevin (*doubtfully*) Really?

Rock Good to breathe fresh air again and feel free
to –

  A burst of gunfire.

Get down!

  They both hurl themselves to the ground.

Kevin Now what do we do?

Rock Keep down, keep your head down . . . (*He
cautiously raises his head. A burst of gunfire. He
flattens himself immediately.*) What are we going
to do?

Kevin Can you shoot back?

Rock No.

Kevin Don't you have your .45?

Rock No.

Kevin Or your .38?

Rock No.

Kevin Or your .22?

Rock No. They took them all off me. I don't even have a pocket-knife. Listen, we'll crawl along the roof here, try and find a way down. Follow me. We stay here, we're sitting ducks. They'll pick us off like dead owls.

More gunfire.

Come on!

They start to crawl.

If I know my old disused warehouses, there's bound to be a flight of emergency stairs or even – at a pinch – a –

Kevin Rockfist, look out!

Rock (*as he falls*) – skyl – i – i – i – g – h – t – t – t!!!!

A silence.
   Kevin peers into the hole through which Rockfist has fallen.

Kevin (*tentatively*) Rockfist!

A groan from Rockfist below.

Are you all right?

Rock Yeah, great. Don't worry about me, kid. I'm made of – titanium. (*He winces with pain. Struggling to his feet*) Come on, what are you waiting for?

Kevin Down there?

Rock Unless you want to stay up there.

More gunfire.

Kevin Here I come.

Kevin jumps.

Rock Nice jumping, kid, now let's get out of here . . .

Kevin Which way?

Rock Who cares? Any way, so long as it's out.

They start to move off. Monique appears and blocks their path. She is French, beautiful, villainous and holds a gun.

Monique *Monsieur Rockfist Slim, quel pleasant surprise.*

Rock Uh – uh!

Kevin (*under his breath*) It's Monique, deadly number-one henchperson of the Green Shark.

Monique Please. Don't run away. We still have things to discuss, *non*?

Rock I've nothing to talk to you about, Monique. Now get out of our way.

Monique Aren't you going to introduce me to your young *ami*? Your friend?

Rock Monique, this is Keith –

Kevin Kevin . . .

Rock He's just a kid, you don't want him. Let him go, huh?

Monique I think *non*, Monsieur Slim. Any friend of yours, I'm sure, must be a friend of ours.

Rock Run for it, kid, just run for it . . .

Kevin But what about you . . .?

Rock You heard me, run!

Kevin runs off in another direction but collides with Brunt, one of Monique's henchmen. Brunt chuckles, holding Kevin firmly.

Monique *Non, non, s'il vous plaît.* I insist you stay.

Kevin I know who you are. You're Monique La Sleek. A blackmailer, thief and murderer.

Monique (*bowing slightly*) Also please, forger, bank robber and *extortioniste*. At your service, young Keith.

Kevin Kevin.

Rock Let the kid go, Monique. You're already facing forty-two charges of murder, you want to add him to the list? You want to deal with someone, you deal with me, OK?

Monique *Hélas, ce n'est pas possible* – not possible, *je regrette*. The Green Shark is most anxious to meet you both.

Rock Is he?

Kevin We're going to meet the Green Shark?

Monique A great honour, yes? There is, unfortunately one small – what you say – snag. Being a very private person, once you have met face to face, the Shark also insists that you die. *Je regrette*, sadly one of the rules of the house. Come now. The car is waiting outside. (*to Brunt, in some unrecognizable tongue*) *Pristo beggini*, Brunt!

Brunt *Beggini pristo*.

Monique After you, *Monsieur Slim*. I will enjoy watching you die.

Rock You're a charmer, Monique. Remind me to marry you sometime and live miserably ever after.

Monique laughs. They start to leave. Kevin wriggles free from Brunt by stamping on his foot. Monique is distracted.

Monique *Sacré*. Stop him! *Shakka bakkar!*

Rockfist knocks the gun out of her hand.

Rock Good boy! Go for it, Kieron!

Kevin (*running*) Kevin!

Brunt (*pursuing him*) *Coot huch! Coot huch!*

Rock (*blocking Brunt's path*) Oh no, you don't! Take that, my friend!

He lands a punch on Brunt, who staggers back, recovers and swings a counter-blow which Rockfist parries.

Brunt *Zurt!*

17

Rock (*to Kevin*) Get the gun, kid! (*to Brunt*) Oh, you want to play that game, huh. You asked for it, my friend!

Rockfist and Brunt carry the fight offstage, still trading blows.
Kevin and Monique simultaneously dive for the gun. They wrestle for possession.

Monique (*as they struggle*) *Ah, non, non, non.* Little boys should not – play – with – guns . . .

Kevin bites her hand.

(*in pain*) Ah! *Mon dieu!*

Kevin has the gun and points it at her.

Kevin All right. Get back. Just get back.

Monique *Donnez-le-moi!* Give it to me!

Kevin I don't want to hurt anyone, just let us go, do you hear?

Monique (*advancing calmly*) Give the gun to me . . .

Kevin Get back! I'm warning you!

Monique *Donnez moi.*

Kevin *Non.* I mean, no.

Monique Give it to me! You either shoot me or give the gun to me. You can't shoot me, you know you can't, so give it to me.

18

A moment of impasse. Rockfist, somewhat dishevelled, appears behind Kevin.

Rock Give it to me, kid. I'll shoot her if necessary.

Kevin (*relieved*) Rockfist. Here! (*He hands the gun to Rockfist.*)

Rock Thanks, kid. Nice work. (*waving the gun at Monique*) Now beat it, *Madame*, before I start shooting.

Monique hesitates.

I said beat it. Go tell your boss you failed.

Monique reluctantly retreats.

Monique (*to Kevin, dangerously*) You, I will remember, little boy. We will meet again, never fear. *Je reviens.* (*She goes.*)

Rock (*after her*) Not if I can help it, you won't! (*to Kevin*) You OK, kid?

Kevin I think so.

Rock Then let's go. Which way's your home?

Kevin I don't know.

Rock You don't know? Terrific. All right. Eeny . . . meeny . . . (*making a random choice*) This way!

Kevin Are you sure?

Rock No. But home is any direction she ain't, my friend. Follow on.

They rush out. There is a whirl of sound and light and we are very definitely in a new location. The floor is marked with several large light and dark squares, like a chess board. It is a chess board.

Rockfist and Kevin return immediately.

(*staring around incredulously*) What the heck . . .? Where are we now?

Kevin I've no idea. This is your story. You should know.

Rock I've never seen this place before in my life . . . How did we get here?

Kevin We sort of – went through a wall – only it wasn't a wall . . . It couldn't have been a wall because it wasn't really there.

Rock You reckon we went through a wall that wasn't there?

Kevin Seemed to.

Rock Terrific. Tell you something, why don't you be a kid that isn't there, then I can get on with my story. We've got – (*consulting his watch*) – sixty-seven hours till the end of the world and we're walking through invisible walls.

Kevin It isn't my fault.

Rock Right now, kid, everything's your fault.

Kevin If it hadn't been for me, you'd still be in that smelting oven . . .

Rock Nuts! I'd have got out of that –

Kevin How?

Rock Somehow! Don't you worry. I'm made of granite . . .

Kevin If it hadn't been for me, Monique would have shot us . . .

Rock (*over him*) Oh, strudel-cake! I'd have fixed her, don't you worry . . .

Kevin (*over him*) If it hadn't been for me –

Rock (*over him*) If it hadn't been for you we wouldn't be standing here somewhere in the middle of nowhere, wondering where the hell we are.

They pause for breath.

Kevin Well, there's no point in arguing.

Rock Who's arguing?

Kevin We are.

Rock No, we're not.

Kevin Yes, we are.

Rock No, we're not.

Kevin Oh, this is stupid. I'm not arguing.

Rock You just said you were.

Kevin Listen, we'd better keep going . . .

Rock How do we keep going if we don't know where we're going?

Kevin What do you suggest, that we just stand here?

Rock Well, it's better than walking around in circles, which is what we'll be doing if we can't figure the straight line.

Kevin At least we'll be going somewhere. If we just stay here –

Rock We're arguing again.

Kevin I know.

Slight pause.

Let's see if we can find someone we can ask.

Rock Ask what?

Kevin Where we are.

Rock The only person we're liable to find is Monique. Which would not be good news. Especially for you, kid. She is not a dame to mess with, I assure you.

Kevin I know . . .

Rock She can kill you thirty-six different ways she chooses and none of them are good and all of them are slow.

Kevin You think she'll come after us?

Rock You'd better believe it. Why, in *The Case of the Poisonous Piranha*, she –

Kevin All the more reason to keep moving, then. Come on.

A White Pawn enters in a hurry. He sees them.

Rock (*seeing him*) What the –? (*He draws his gun.*) Hold it right there!

Pawn (*agitated*) What do you here? What do you here, you pair?

Rock Hold it right there, mister!

Pawn (*ignoring him entirely*) The battle now is all but lost. That way!

Kevin Battle?

Pawn
What do you off your squares? Resume thy posts!
I beg thee to return unto thy squares!

Rock To our what?

Pawn
The battle's all but lost! Your squares, my lords!
Lest we lose everything in one foul swoop!

Kevin Sorry?

Rock Who is this guy?

Pawn
One Castle, one brave Bishop and three Pawns

Have lately been dispatched. I fear the Queen
Will shortly follow; I must call her now!

Kevin I don't know what he's talking about.

Rock I think I'm going to shoot him!

Pawn (*suddenly, urgently*) Watch to thy backs!
(*He pushes them back into a corner.*)

Rock What are you –!

Pawn I do beseech thee hush!

*A moment and then a Red Bishop appears. He
is reading a book and is deep in thought. He
travels diagonally across the floor, humming to
himself. He fails to notice them but goes
straight off in the other direction.*

(*in a muted voice*) 'Tis the Red King's Bishop . . .

Rock (*loudly*) What did he say –!

Kevin and Pawn Sssshh!

Pawn The danger's passed. Praise God he did not
see.

Rock Who was that guy? He looked like some
crazy priest.

Pawn 'Twas the Red King's Bishop. Curse the day.

Kevin (*thoughtfully*) The Red King's Bishop . . .

Rock Does the guy spell trouble?

Pawn

He has now ended five good lives today.
I do not doubt he will take more e'er long . . .

Rock A serial killer bishop? I don't believe it.

Pawn

Yet there is one far deadlier than he;
Red Gareth, fearful horseman to the king,
Who single-handed hath bedrenched this board
With White Pawn's noble blood. He rides this
    way . . .

Rock Red *Gareth*?

Pawn

I bid thee farewell, friends, I cannot stay.
The Queen doth need her subjects all this day,
If she is not to perish with the rest.
Go forward and God speed, may your resolve,
Turn this sad morn to joyous eventide.
Adieu!

The Pawn departs.

Rock He's a lunatic! The guy's a lunatic.

Kevin Rockfist!

Rock Get me out of here! Somebody help!

Kevin Rockfist! I think I know where we are.

Rock So do I. We're in a lunatic asylum . . .

Kevin No, no. We're not. I think we've . . . somehow changed books.

Rock Changed books? What are you talking about, changed books?

Kevin We're – it's hard to explain .... We're no longer in *Rockfist Slim and the Case of the Green Shark*. We've crossed into – something else.

Rock Kid, you've lost me. Have you caught the local disease? Just give me a plain answer. Do you know where we are, yea or nay?

Kevin Yea. Yes.

Rock Where are we?

Kevin We're in *Chess for Beginners*.

Rock *Chess for Beginners*?

Kevin Listen, when I put the book away – your book, as it were – I put it next to another book on the same shelf –

Rock Next to *Chess for Beginners*?

Kevin Yes.

Rock Which we're now in?

Kevin Yes.

Rock But how did we get here?

Kevin I don't know.

Rock I'm a private eye. I'm supposed to be discovering the identity of the Green Shark – I have (*consulting his watch*) – sixty-six hours, twenty-three

26

minutes till he intends to destroy the world and now I'm in a book on chess being threatened by a guy called Red Gareth. If the world ends, kid, I am holding you solely responsible, OK?

Kevin Yep. Sorry.

Rock Well, there's nothing for it, I guess. We'd better keep going. We've got black Monique behind us, not to mention the killer Bishop and Red Gareth in front of us. It seems to me we should have stayed in the oven, kid . . .

Kevin Maybe we ought to . . .

Rock What?

Kevin Well, that one mistook us for pawns, didn't he? Like him.

Rock He did?

Kevin Maybe we should move like pawns. So as not to draw attention.

Rock How does one move like a pawn, prithee?

Kevin One square at a time. That's how pawns move, didn't you know that?

Rock How should I? I'm allergic to all sea food . . .

Kevin Pawns, not prawns. All right, let's do it. One square at a time, right?

Rock After you.

We imagine at this point that the stage is divided into thirty squares, five across (A–E) and six down (1–6). At the start, Kevin is standing on square B1 and Rockfist on C1.

Kevin (*moving forward to B2*) One . . .

Rock (*moving forward to C2*) One . . . This could take us a year.

Kevin (*moving forward to B3*) Two . . . Keep going.

Rock Tell me, do pawns have a long life expectancy? (*moving diagonally to D3*) Two . . .

Kevin No. Not diagonally. Only forwards. Pawns only move forwards. They only move diagonally when they're taking something . . .

Rock Taking somethin'? What do you mean, like when they're shoplifting?

Kevin No. Not . . . Never mind. Just move for-wards, all right?

Rock If you say so, kid. As my pa used to say, if you find yourself in a madhouse, you might as well get friendly with the madmen. (*He moves to his correct square, C3.*) How many more of these squares?

Kevin Altogether there's sixty-four.

Rock We'll be old men . . .

Kevin No, eight. We only need to cover eight. With any luck we should be –

He breaks off as a horse's screaming whinnying is heard. Suddenly Red Gareth appears on square A6. He is a very sinister apparition. A horseback figure, entirely in red, upon a red horse. His face is hidden by a visor. He holds a large sword.

Rock (*in a low voice*) Oh, my God!

Gareth laughs a sinister laugh. He studies them. His horse neighs eagerly.

Gareth
Whooaa there, Hemlock! What knaves are these,
    think'st thou,
Who block our path? Obstruct us in this way?

Rock You think I should shoot him?

Kevin No, wait! We're safe at the moment.

Rock We are?

Kevin He can't take us from where he is at present.

Rock I stand to be convinced by your argument. What makes you think so?

Kevin Because his horse can only move two squares forward and one to the side . . .

Rock You're kidding?

Kevin Or else one square forward and two to the side. You understand?

Rock I understand entirely. I regularly bet on ones just like it.

Gareth Your move, my little lords. Come, clear the way!

Rock What do we do now?

Kevin We'll – we'll try and outmanoeuvre him.

Rock Kid, I hate to worry you but this is one big man in a tin suit on a large horse with a very big sword. I don't fancy the odds. Two to the side or not, I'm shooting him.

Kevin Wait! Stay where you are. You heard him, it's our move. I'm going to move forward one square. You stay where you are.

Rock You know what you're doing?

Kevin I hope so.

Gareth Move!

Rock Hang on! Kid, wait a second! You say you're going to move forward one square?

Kevin Yes.

Rock But then if he moves – let's see – two squares and one to the side – then he can take you. The guy can take you.

Kevin He could, except, if he did, then you can take him.

Rock Oh, yeah. Still, what good's that to you?

Kevin I don't think he'll risk it. We're only pawns to him. He's a knight. He wouldn't sacrifice himself for a pawn. (*sotto*) I hope.

Gareth Move!

Kevin Here I go.

He moves forward to square B4. Gareth's horse whinnies.

That's got him worried.

Rock It's got his horse worried, anyway.

Kevin Now, if he tries to take me, you'll take him. If he makes the other move, I'll take him.

Rock (*studying this*) I reconsider my opinion. You're one smart kid.

Kevin (*to Gareth*) Your move, my lord.

Rock Your move, sucker.

The Red Bishop appears on C1 behind them.

Uh-uh. Bad news, kid. The church militant is back.

Gareth Thy move.

Bishop Thy move.

Kevin Our move.

Rock Don't look at me.

Kevin OK. I'm going to move forward one more square. Try and put him under pressure.

He moves forward again to square B5. The horse whinnies.

Rock Nice going, kid. Heyyy!

He reacts as, quite suddenly, Gareth moves with a flourish from A6 to C5.

What now?

Kevin It's all right, we're still safe. Just keep an eye on that Bishop.

Rock Any guy in a frock like that, I'm watching like a hawk.

Kevin I'm going to move another square.

Rock Careful, kid.

Kevin It's OK. Here I go.

Kevin moves from B5 to B6.

Rock I get a feeling of being left behind here. I don't mind, you understand, it's just kind of lonely. Out here in the middle of a battlefield with only a bloodstained horse and a mad bishop for –

The Bishop moves from C1 to D2, thus endangering Rockfist.

Kevin Rockfist! Watch the Bishop!

Rockfist turns to find himself nose to nose with the Bishop.

Rock Oh, hi. Good afternoon, your worshipful –

eminence, sir – or madam. Get me out of here, kid, I need some advice. This guy looks set to eat his entire flock –

Kevin It's all right. Just move one square forward. You'll be perfectly safe.

Rock One square forward. That puts me awful close to the mad Horseman, kid.

Kevin Take your pick.

Rock Oh, well. At least the horse is a vegetarian. I trust. (*He moves from C3 to C4.*) Mission accomplished.

Gareth moves again from C5 to A4. He laughs.

Gareth Thy move.

Kevin Oh, no. I think he's got me. I'm sorry.

Rock Not quite, kid. Stand by for the master move. I've got you covered, never fear . . .

Kevin No, Rockfist, I wouldn't do that, I really –

Rockfist has moved forward from C4 to C5.

Rock OK, Gareth, your move.

Bishop But nay, my lord, my move it is, I trust. (*He moves from D2 to E3.*)

Gareth Thy move.

Bishop Thy move.

Kevin (*worried*) Oh, dear . . .

Rock Now, I know I'm only just beginning to get the hang of this game, but this appears to me to be the situation. Correct me if I'm wrong. At the present moment, both you and I can be taken by the horse. In addition, if I move forward you can also be taken by the Bishop. If, on the other hand, I do not move forward I can be taken by the Bishop. Either way, one of us, possibly both, are dead men. Therefore, I am drawn to the conclusion, to hell with strategy, the only way out of here is for me to start shooting. Beginning with the Bishop. Stand back. (*He produces Monique's gun and points it at the Bishop.*) I'm sorry, reverend. Many apologies. (*He fires the gun. It clicks, but does not fire.*) I should have known better than to shoot at a bishop.

He clicks it some more at Gareth. Kevin ducks.

What's wrong with this thing? It's full of bullets.

Kevin I don't think it'll work here. It belongs in your book, you see. Not this one. In chess there aren't any guns.

Rock (*resigned*) In that case, I'll take the horse, you take the Bishop. At least we'll go down fighting. Been good knowing you. (*He extends his hand.*)

Kevin Been good knowing you, Rockfist. I'm sorry I didn't manage to –

Rock Kid, don't blame yourself, you're a genius.

Me, I'd have been finished on square one, back there. Don't blame yourself. All right, you guys. We decided we ain't going to move.

Gareth
You needs must move, my lords . . .

Bishop
. . . you needs must move!

Rock You want us, come and get us.

Gareth Thy move!

Rock No, thy move!

Bishop Nay, thy move.

Rock Nay, thy move!

Kevin Thy move!

Rock Thy move!

Gareth and Bishop Thy move!

The White Queen enters at C1. She is very impressive.

Queen My move, methinks, Lord Bishop, by my troth.

She bears down on the Bishop. The Bishop throws up his hands.

Bishop Aaaaaaahhhh!!!!

The Queen arrives at E3 and destroys him. (Somehow.)

Rock Hey! Some dame.

Kevin (*awed*) It's the Queen.

Queen (*to Gareth*)
Your move, Sir Knight. But truly have a care,
These gentlemen by me are rendered safe.
And I here warrant, if you value life,
Thou should'st consider flight the safer course
Than doing battle with a queen whose blood,
A tide of fury at thy earlier deeds,
Still courses through these royal veins. Begone!

Gareth's horse whinnies.

Rock Jeez! This dame's tougher than my ex-wife.

*Gareth considers the options. In the end he
chooses the safer course and moves from A4 to
B2.*
   The Queen moves from E3 to D4.

Queen Thy move!

*Gareth selects his only option and gallops to D1
and then off and beyond.*

Begone! (*half to herself*) I fear he will return.

Rock Ma'am, we're – er – My name is Rockfist
Slim, this is young Kelly –

Kevin Kevin –

Rock We're both – er – it's hard to say this, ma'am
– where I come from, most of the time – it's the

dames that need rescuing – if you get my meaning
– but you just about turned the tables there, ma'am
– I mean, don't get me wrong, I'm certainly not saying there ain't dames who – er – women – ladies –
who can – I know one in particular – but I have to
say I guess you're just about the biscuit-taking lolla-
palulu there.

Queen (*to Kevin*) What say'st thy friend?

Kevin He thankest thee, Your Majesty. As I. Do.

Queen
  And I thee, Crispin. Strangers that thou art,
  Thou hast no spur to fight our noble cause.

Kevin Happy we are to help – indeed we, ma'am.

Rock Yea! Could'st thou directeth us, please? We
seeketh the path to take yon lad home.

Queen What say'st he? Home? Where dwell'st
thou, Crispin, pray?

Rock Kelvin.

Kevin
  Kevin. My home is – hard to show. It lies beyond
  The borders of this land . . . in Surbiton.

Queen
  I know not Surbiton. (*indicating*) But choose
    that path.
  For northwards do our peaceful borders lie.
  The South is fraught with hazards yet, I fear.

I would direct no honest stranger there.

Kevin And East and West? What's there?

Queen
> I know them not.
> We have no East or West. They are that place
> Where wretched souls of those departed dwell.
> I must be gone for I am needed now.
> My thanks again, I wish thy journey speed.
> A safe return to Surbiton. Farewell!

She moves off at great speed.

Kevin Farewell!

Rock Farewell! (*watching her go*) I think I may be in love. But I guess I'm not her type. How would she adapt to a cold-water apartment in the Bronx? Bad plumbing, roaches and rats. That's not for her. Besides we have – (*consulting his watch*) – sixty-two hours till meltdown, kid. I need to get you home, look at that book and identify the Green Shark . . . why are we hanging around here?

Kevin We're waiting till you've stopped talking.

Rock OK, I'm done. Which way's the bedroom?

Kevin Northwards, she said. Her guess is as good as ours. That way.

Rock Then follow on'st, my lord.

Kevin Rockfist.

Rock What?

G

Kevin Do you think Monique's following us?

Rock I wouldn't be surprised. Hopefully she'll meet with the Queen. That could be an interesting confrontation. Come on! Next stop, your bedroom. Chin up, kid, we're nearly there.

He goes off, Kevin follows.
Scarcely have they gone when Monique appears. She is whistling to herself. She is swinging something in her hand. It's Gareth's visor. She holds it up and admires it. She follows on after Rockfist and Kevin.
The moment she is gone, the lights change and we are in a deep forest. Birdsong, dappled sunlight.
Kevin and Rockfist reappear. They stop.

(*over the birdsong*) Is this your bedroom?

Kevin I don't have trees growing in my bedroom.

Rock Just a long shot. You're a weird enough kid.

Kevin Listen, would you mind calling me Kevin?

Rock Sure.

Kevin I mean, not Kerry or Keith or Calvin and especially not kid. Kevin, my name's Kevin!

Rock (*reasonably*) OK. KEVIN!

Kevin Thank you!

Rock You've only got to say.

Kevin Right!

Rock Kevin. There you are! Whatever makes you happy, kid.

Kevin gives up.

So, where are we now? Do you recognize it?

Kevin (*shaking his head*) No. It's just a forest. It could be anywhere.

Rock What books have you got with forests in them?

Kevin I don't know.

Rock Well, think of the books on your shelves.

Kevin I'm trying. There are dozens.

Rock Dozens? (*looking at his watch*) Listen, I can't spend time going through dozens of books, I've got – fifty-four hours – fifty-four? What's the matter with this watch? It was sixty-two hours a minute ago.

Kevin We may be moving through different time zones.

Rock Oh, yeah? How do you know?

Kevin Just a theory.

Rock What I'm saying is, if you've got dozens of books on your shelf, we may as well give up now.

Kevin No, I have dozens of books, yes – well,

quite a lot – but not all on that particular shelf.

Rock So how many you got on this particular shelf?

Kevin I can't remember. Six? A dozen?

Rock If there's only six, how come you can't remember the damn titles?

Kevin (*distressed*) I'm sorry.

Rock (*soothingly*) OK, OK. Just do your best to remember. It's important, you see. If we both want to get through here, you need to remember the titles. I mean we could be anywhere from *Huckleberry Finn* to *The Boys' Book of Nature Walks*.

Kevin I know that. Don't you think I'm trying? It's difficult. I bet you can't remember all the books on your shelves.

Rock I don't have any books. I don't even have any shelves.

Kevin What do you read?

Rock The *Daily News*. Then I use it to wrap up the cat litter.

Kevin You've got a cat?

Rock A stray. He's called Armageddin.

Kevin Armageddin?

Rock On account of give me the food and then Armageddin out of here.

41

A little man appears, some distance from them.
He hops about on one leg, gleefully.

Man
Today I bake, tomorrow I brew,
The next I'll have the young Queen's child.
Ha! Glad I am that no one knew,
That Rumpelstiltskin I am styled.

He goes off.

Rock What in the heck –?

Kevin That's where we are!

Rock Where?

Kevin *Grimm's Fairy Tales.*

Rock *Grimm's Fairy Tales?* Plural? How many of those are there?

Kevin Hundreds. You must know them. *Sleeping Beauty, Cinderella, Rumpelstiltskin, Hansel and Gretel, Snow White, The Frog Prince* . . .

Rock Hold it! Hold it! Hold it! We got to go through all those?

Kevin I hope not.

Rock So do I. Or we're in deep trouble. There's just so many dancing gnomes and sleeping princesses I can take before I start shooting.

Kevin I don't think your gun's going to work here either, somehow. Let's try and find someone, shall we?

Rock We'd better. Before Monique finds us.

Kevin You really think she's after us?

Rock Bet your life on it, she's back there somewhere.

Kevin Why's she bothering with us?

Rock Because you bit her hand and I know too much. Come on.

They walk a bit.

This forest just goes on and on.

They walk a bit.

We could be in here for ever.

They walk a bit.

We could even be going in circles.

They walk a bit.

How are we to know? Look, that's the same tree we just passed a minute ago. It's smiling at us. I'd know that smile –

Kevin Look!

Rock What?

Kevin Can you see? Through the trees. It's a cottage. In the clearing.

Rock Oh, yeah. Let's go see.

They reach the cottage.

Kevin Are you going to knock?

Rock You knock. I'll keep you covered.

Kevin knocks. They listen. He knocks again.

(*nervously*) Nobody in. Let's go.

Kevin Wait! (*calling*) Hallo! Anyone home?

He tries the door handle. The door creaks open.

Rock What you doing?

Kevin It's open.

Rock Come on, let's get out of here.

Kevin Are you nervous?

Rock I'm not nervous.

Kevin You're nervous!

Rock All right, I'm nervous. I'm not used to this. Forests and cottages. I'm used to sleazy bars and crummy hotels and traffic fumes and mean streets. I'm not used to this.

Kevin Come on. Let's look inside.

Rock Kid, listen. I might not read much but I do know this. In these kind of stories no good comes of pushing your way into cottages in the middle of deep woods. Because in my experience, twenty minutes later three angry bears show up and start kicking up hell.

44

Kevin Come on.

Rock OK. Just don't touch the porridge.

They enter the cottage, cautiously.

Kevin (*calling*) Hallo! Anybody home?

They listen.

It's completely deserted.

Rock The seven dwarves are at work. Let's go. We can catch up with that little hopping guy. Ask him.

Kevin I wonder if there's any food.

Rock Don't touch the food! I told you, you're not to touch the food!

Kevin Why not? I'm hungry.

Rock You eat it, you'll turn into something. Or you'll shrink.

Kevin Shrink?

Rock You'll be two inches high going through little tiny doors and meet caterpillars . . .

Kevin That's *Alice in Wonderland*.

Rock I don't care. These things happen. These are dangerous places, kid. Once you start, before you know it you're kissing frogs, ugly ducks are quacking and dogs are singing and you're getting glued to golden geese. I tell you, in this place, the giants aren't far away.

Kevin Wait there. I'm going to find the kitchen. (*He moves away.*)

Rock Crazy! The kid's crazy . . .

An old woman appears behind him. She stands watching him. Rockfist becomes aware of her.

(*out of the corner of his mouth*) Kid . . . hey, kid . . . Kilroy. Hey!

Kevin What?

Rock Behind me. There's someone behind me, there. D'you see?

Kevin Oh, hallo. Sorry, we – didn't know you were at home.

Woman
Hallo, my friends, please have no fear,
For you are very welcome here.

Rock Thanks a lot. All we really want are some directions, ma'am. If you could help us at all we'd be most grateful.

Woman
Both eat and drink what you require,
And warm yourselves beside the fire.

Rock Why don't she answer me? Are we into the land of more peculiar talking?

Kevin I've just remembered. It was a verse book.

Rock A what book?

Kevin Grimm's fairy tales in verse. They all talked in verse.

Woman
Do come inside and take a seat.
My granddaughter you soon can meet.

Rock You mean we have to talk like her.

Kevin That may be the only way she'll understand us. (*He clears his throat.*)
We – thank you, lady, very much.
We do not need that much, as such.

Woman
I'm certain you require some tea,
Please come this way and follow me.

She moves inside. They follow. They enter a confined space. They are jammed together.

Kevin
This room that's leading off the hall.
It seems to me to be quite small.

Woman
Oh, silly me! The dining room!
This is the place I keep the broom.

She leads them into the dining room.

Rock
I don't want you to panic, lad,
It seems to me she's barking mad.

Woman

Now please sit down, do take a seat
I'll find you something both to eat.
The kitchen must be somewhere near.
I'll cook a meal and bring it here.

Rock

Oh, goody, goody, thank you so –
I think though that it's time to go.

Woman

Just sit and wait there patiently,
Unless you want to anger me.

Kevin

I wonder, madam, if perhaps,
You have such things as local maps?

Rock Good, kid.

Woman

You will not need a map or charts,
To find your way around these parts.
Be back before you count to ten – (*She makes to leave.*)
Whoops! That's the cupboard once again.

She goes out.

Rock

I don't want you to worry, but
I think we're trapped here with a nut.

Kevin I'm still trying to think what story this must be . . .

Rock
  We both must be upon our metal,
  She may think I'm Hansel, you are Gretel . . .

Kevin It's OK, we don't have to talk like that, now.

Rock Oh, sure. I forgot.

Kevin Only to talk to her. On the other hand, if
we don't talk in rhyme, she won't know what
we're saying.

Rock Which could be useful if the going gets
tough. Meanwhile, who is she? Any clues?

Kevin Well, she's not the witch from Hansel and
Gretel. Otherwise this house would be made out of
gingerbread.

Rock There's no sign of a bear and she certainly
ain't Snow White. Rumpelstiltskin's mother? Nah.
Hey, wait a minute, didn't she say something about
meeting a granddaughter?

Kevin That's right. Now who has a grandmother?

Both (*simultaneously*) Little Red Riding Hood!

Rock Do you think that's her grandmother? The
one that gets eaten by the . . .

Kevin Possibly. Unless. Unless she's already been
eaten by the . . .

Rock In which case, that's the . . .

Kevin Which would explain why she doesn't

49

know her way round her own house.

The Woman returns with a tray. On it are two glasses of lemonade, a teapot and two cups.

Woman
Do please excuse me, gentlemen,
I could not find this room again.
The larder's empty I'm afraid.
Just biscuits and some lemonade.
And as a little treat for me,
A dainty cup of jasmine tea.

Kevin
Much as we'd really like to stay –

Rock
I guess we must be on our way –

Woman
No, no, this lemon drink is yours.
I squeezed them with my own two – hands.

Rock Don't touch the drink! She's spiked it.

Woman
My granddaughter is here at nine,
With cherry cake and home-made wine.

Kevin It's her!

Woman
To miss her would be such a loss.
Besides you'll make me very cross.
Now drink it. Eat the biscuits, too.
Or it will be the worse for you.

Kevin What do we do?

Rock Stall for time. We'll jump her when she's distracted.

Kevin She's a wolf!

Rock
Tell me – mmm! This biscuit's good! –
Your grandkid's not Red Riding Hood?

Woman (*suspiciously*)
How did you know that was her name?
I want to know just why you came?

Kevin Now you've done it.

Rock
I'm sorry, you've not understood.
I knew her dad, Jim Riding Hood.
He used to be an old school chum.
And that's the reason that we – come.

(*to Kevin*) Let's go!

Woman
Sit down! I won't be disobeyed!
And drink that glass of lemonade.
It is my special home-made brew.
You'll find it strangely good for you.

She pushes back her bonnet to reveal two large ears. She snarls slightly.

Rock Here come the ears.

Kevin What are we going to do?

Rock I don't know about you but bottoms up, old bean! (*He raises the glass.*)

Kevin It's probably poisoned.

The Wolf snarls.

Rock You gonna argue with that thing?

Kevin Oh, well. Been nice knowing you . . .

They raise their glasses and prepare to drink.
A loud knock on the door.

Wolf
Oh, good gracious, to be sure!
My evening meal is at the door.
Now, not one word from you or him –
Or I will tear you limb from limb.

The Wolf moves to the door.

Rock It's not altogether surprising that wolves are an endangered species.

Wolf (*calling through the doorway*)
My dear, you're just in time for tea,
Your granny has some company.

The Wolf has turned away for a second. Kevin empties both their glasses into the Wolf's teapot. Little Red Riding Hood enters. She carries a basket.

R-Hood

Forgive me, I'm a little late.
I'm sorry if I made you wait.
I met a stranger in the wood –
Good day, my name is Riding Hood.
Though, gentlemen, you can instead,
If you prefer, just call me Red.
Oh Grandmama, you've such big ears,
I never noticed, all these years.
And gracious! What a big surprise!
You've also got enormous eyes.
And great big hands and, oh, good grief,
You've also got enormous teeth.

Wolf

Sit down, my dearest, next to me.
And let me pour you out some tea.

Rock Uh-uh. There goes plan A.

Wolf (*pouring tea*)

We surely change, with every breath,
The closer that we get to death.
It's true for me, it's true for you,
I think you'll find you do so, too.
Here, take this cup and share with me
Some nice refreshing jasmine tea.

R-Hood

Oh, this looks lovely. Did I say?
I met a wolf back there today. (*She goes to drink.*)

Rock

> Before you drink that, may I state,
> Our lemonade just then was great.

Wolf (*sipping tea*)

> How nice to have one's work admired –
> You may now feel a little tired . . .

Kevin

> A trifle sleepy. (*to R-Hood*) Tell us more
> About this wolf you said you saw.

R-Hood (*who was about to drink*)

> Well, mama would have been annoyed,
> She told me wolves were to avoid . . .

Rock (*laughing*)

> I guess a wolf's a bit like men,
> You're safe enough with one in ten . . .

Wolf (*sipping tea, glaring at them*)

> Now please remember what I said.
> Do both feel free to go to bed . . .

R-Hood

> Why I should fear them, I don't know,
> I found him very friendly though . . .
> > (*she goes to drink.*)

Kevin (*preventing her*)

> Please, tell me something, if you could,
> Your uncle isn't Robin Hood?

R-Hood

> I do not think so. Who is he?

Wolf (*snarling*)

Just let her drink her jasmine tea . . .
Look, leave the girl with me, you two,
I have some cooking I must do.

R-Hood

Oh, granny, may I come and look –
Or maybe even help you cook?
What is it that you're going to make?

Wolf (*increasingly agitated*)

A tender juicy braising steak . . .
With roast potatoes, peas and beans,
Thick onion gravy, sprouts and greens,
With Yorkshire puddings, specially made,
All in a jasmine marinade.
And afterwards a . . . a . . . a . . . a . . .

The Wolf sways uncertainly and collapses.

R-Hood

Oh, goodness, come and help me, chaps,
What's made my grandmama collapse?

Rock This girl's beyond belief.
(*to R-Hood*) This ain't your gran, kid, it's not her,
Unless she's grown a coat of fur.
This is a wolf, the one you met –
It beats me how you could forget . . .

R-Hood

Well, how was I supposed to guess
When he is wearing Granny's dress?
Where's Granny, then?

Kevin
  I think she's dead.

Rock
  He ate her whilst she lay in bed.

  Riding Hood collapses.

Tough break. Come on, let's shift the wolf.

Kevin You don't think . . .?

Rock Think what?

Kevin That the grandmother's still inside the wolf?
She is in the story. They cut the wolf open and
there's the grandmother still alive.

Rock You want to do that?

Kevin Not much.

Rock You want to fish around in this wolf for a
partially digested grandmother? If she's still alive in
there, I prefer not to meet her. Grab a paw.

  They drag the Wolf off.

(*to Riding Hood, as they do this*) Hey, kid, can we
send for someone to look after you?

  No reply.

Hey! You listenin'?

Kevin She can't hear you . . .
  Is there someone who lives near,
  Who we could fetch for you – my dear?

R-Hood
My own house isn't all that far,
I'll run back home to my mama,
Once I have cleaned this house right through.
Dear Granny would have liked me to.
But first I'll have a little cry,
I thank you, both of you, goodbye.

She goes off tearfully.

Rock Let's get out of this place, I'm running out of rhymes.

Kevin We still don't know which way.

Rock Let's face it, we never know which way. This whole journey is lousy guesswork. We're jumping blind from book to book. We've no idea what's ahead. We only got to hit a dictionary next and we're dead men.

Riding Hood appears at the window.

R-Hood
Grandma's alive! We should have guessed!
He locked her in the linen chest!
Oh, happy day! Oh glory be!
I'll pour her out some jasmine tea.

Rock Oh, my God! Not the tea!

Kevin
No, not the tea! Give her the wine.
I think you'll find she – will be fine.

Riding Hood makes to go in.

Please, could you tell us, if indeed
You know, which way these roads both lead?

R-Hood
To my own cottage that path goes –
The other, that way no one knows.
Though people say, just round that bend,
There's nothing more; this world does end.
I urge you both don't even try . . .
Oh, Granny's calling now. Bye-bye.

Riding Hood goes in.

Rock Bingo! End of the world, Kelvin. Their
world. You hear that? That's got to be the way. I
feel it. Let's get out of here. I won't be sorry not to
hear another rhyming couplet again.
So come on, take my arm here, friend,
Your bedroom's just around that bend!

Kevin OK.

*They both go off triumphantly. A second later
and Monique enters. She is swinging the Wolf's
head and is whistling softly, as before.*

Monique (*in a sing-song voice*) *Ici!* I'm getting
closer . . .

*She goes off after them. As she does so, the scene
changes dramatically. Howling wind and a
dark moonless night.*
  Kevin and Rockfist enter, buffeted by the wind.

Kevin (*over the wind*) Please don't ask me if this is my bedroom . . .

Rock (*likewise*) Where are we now?

Kevin Search me!

Rock We'd better find some shelter. Look, there's a light! Do you see? Way in the distance there. Probably Bluebeard's castle. Come on! Before my butt freezes over.

They walk a few paces.

Kevin There's someone up ahead! Look!

Jennet appears, a lean, sour-faced woman.

Excuse me! Could you tell us where we are? What's that house up ahead?

Jennet (*with malignant anger*) That is the House of Shaws! Blood built it; blood stopped the building of it; blood shall bring it down. See here! I spit upon the ground, and crack my thumb at it! Black be its fall! If ye see the laird, tell him what ye hear; tell him this makes the twelve hunner and nineteen time that Jennet Clouston has called down the curse on him and his house, byre and stable, man, guest, and master, wife, miss, or bairn – black, black be their fall! (*She goes.*)

Rock What did she say?

Kevin (*a little stunned*) Oh, no . . .

Rock Who the heck was that? Where are we?

Kevin We're in *Kidnapped*.

Rock *Kidnapped?* What's *Kidnapped?*

Kevin It's a famous book. By Robert Louis Stevenson. And, believe me, we're in big trouble. (*He starts to move on.*)

Rock (*following him*) What kind of trouble, kid? What kind of trouble?

Kevin You'll see soon enough. Come on!

They go off as the wind howls round them. Blackout.

ACT TWO

The same. Howling wind.
 Kevin and Rockfist enter, pushing against the wind. They reach the front door of the House of Shaws. Kevin bangs on the door. No reply. He bangs again.

Rock There's got to be someone here. There's a light.

Kevin Oh, yes, I remember this bit.

Rock What bit?

Kevin You'll see.

He knocks again.
 Ebenezer appears at the window with a blunderbuss. He is in his nightshirt and night-cap.

Ebenezer It's loaded.

Kevin We have come here with a letter to Mr Ebenezer of Shaws.

Rock We have?

Kevin Is he here?

Ebenezer From whom is it?

Kevin That is neither here nor there.

Ebenezer Well, ye can put it down upon the doorstep, and be off with ye.

Kevin No, I won't. I'm putting it into his hands personally. It's a letter of introduction.

Ebenezer A what?

Kevin A letter of introduction.

Ebenezer Who are ye, yourself?

Kevin My name is – David – er – er . . .

Ebenezer Do ye not ken your ain name?

Kevin Of course I do . . . David – Balmoral.

Ebenezer Who?

Kevin Balfour. That's it. David Balfour.

A pause.

Ebenezer Is your father dead? Ay, he'll be dead no doubt; and that'll be what brings ye chapping to my door. (*Slight pause.*) Well, man, I'll let you in. (*He goes inside.*)

Rock Hey! That was smart. We're in. Whatever you said, we're in.

Kevin It wasn't that smart. I told him I was David Balfour.

Rock And?

Kevin In the next chapter, he tries to kill me.

Rock You think we should be moving along?

Kevin You see anywhere else? It's freezing.

A great rattling of chains and bolts. Finally Ebenezer opens the door to them.

Ebenezer (*looking at Rockfist*) Who's that?

Kevin This is my friend – er – Rocky McSlim.

Ebenezer Oh, aye. Go into the kitchen and touch naething.

Kevin and Rockfist move inside the house. They arrive in a kitchen. Some chairs, a table upon which is a half-eaten bowl of porridge and a small cup of beer. Behind them, more rattling of chains.

Rock Listen, how safe are we if he's trying to kill you?

Kevin I don't think he tries till tomorrow.

Rock You don't *think*? Listen, now we're inside, tell him who we are.

Kevin He'll chuck us out again.

Rock Try chucking me out.

Kevin That's a big gun he's got.

Rock So what? I got a gun. (*He produces it and pulls the trigger.*) Except it still doesn't work.

Kevin Wrong time zone.

Rock Hey, talking of time – (*consulting his watch*) Oh, no, we've done another time leap. We only have thirty-four hours to go. We can't stay here.

Kevin Just till morning, till it's light.

Rock We can't afford to wait, kid.

Kevin We'd never find our way. It's pitch dark out there. No moon, nothing. You fancy a night out there?

Rock All right. As soon as it's light.

Ebenezer rejoins them.

Ebenezer Just locked the door again. Are you sharp-set? Ye can eat that drop parritch?

Rock What's he saying?

Kevin He's offering us his porridge. (*to Ebenezer*) No, thank you, you finish it.

Ebenezer Oh, I can do fine wanting it. I'll take the ale, though, for it slockens my cough. (*He drinks.*)

Rock I can't understand a word he's saying. Slockens his what? What's a slocken?

Ebenezer What's he saying?

Kevin Nothing.

Ebenezer I cannae understand the man at all.

Rock What's he saying?

Kevin He can't understand you.

Rock He can't understand *me*? Well, great. That makes two of us, buddy.

Ebenezer What's he saying?

Kevin Nothing.

Rock What was that?

Kevin Nothing.

   Silence.

Rock Well, that's killed that conversation.

Ebenezer Now you give me that letter, Davie, and sit down and fill your kyte.

Kevin If it's all the same to you, sir, could we do that in the morning? We need to go to bed. We're that – cluffed.

Ebenezer You're what?

Kevin (*to Rockfist*) He wants to see the letter.

Rock Don't give it to him.

Kevin I haven't got one.

Ebenezer So, you're needing your bed?

Kevin Aye.

Ebenezer (*pulling a key from his pocket*) There.

There's the key of the stair tower at the far end of the house. Your room's at the top. (*giving Kevin the key*) Just along the passage there.

Kevin Thank you. Can we have a light?

Ebenezer Hoot-toot, hoot-toot! Lights in a house is a thing I dinnae agree with. I'm unco feared of fires. Goodnight to ye.

Kevin He won't give us a light.

Rock It's pitch dark.

Kevin I know.

Ebenezer The stairs are good but keep to the wall, there's nae banisters. But stairs are grand underfoot.

Kevin Goodnight, then.

Kevin and Rockfist grope their way into the darkness.

Rock I can't see anything. Where are we?

Kevin Just feel the wall. Hold on to me.

They grope along some more. As they climb the wind steadily increases.

Rock How do we know this isn't a trap?

Kevin No, I remember. We're still in Chapter Three. It's tomorrow. He tries to kill Davie tomorrow. He sends him upstairs for some papers.

Rock I hope you're right.

Kevin Hey! Here are the stairs. Remember, keep to the wall, there's no banister rail. Up we go.

Rock Couldn't we sleep on the floor? It's kind of creepy here.

Kevin (*inspired*) Rockfist, your lighter! We can use that.

Rock My lighter! Why didn't I think of that? (*He retrieves it from his pocket and clicks it alight.*)

Kevin That's better.

Rock (*as they proceed*) How do we know there isn't something waiting for us at the top? Or some-one?

A loud, distant knocking.

What the –? What was that?

Kevin No idea. Come on.

Rock I don't like all this.

Kevin I don't remember any knocking in the book. Come on, let's talk about something. Why do you need to know who the Green Shark is? Don't you have enough information to stop him anyway?

Rock No, I don't. His identity is the last missing piece of the jigsaw. If I don't know who he is, we can't locate him, we can't arrest him. Trouble is, nobody knows who he is. I doubt even Monique knows who he is. And there's no one closer to him than Monique.

Kevin I wonder where she is.

Rock Some way behind us, I hope. The only person who knows who the Green Shark is, is you. Only you ain't read the rest of the book yet, so you don't know either. Once we get you back, you can look at the end of the book and tell me who he is, then I can solve it. Trouble is, if Monique's figured that out – and she's smart enough – that puts you in considerable personal danger. But don't worry. You're probably about to get killed by your Uncle Ebenezer, anyway, so then you don't have to worry about her at all. How much higher are we going?

Kevin I don't know.

The lighter suddenly goes out.

What's happened?

Rock Wind blew it out, that's all. Hang on.

Kevin (*cheerfully continuing*) No, I think we must be getting very near to the top, I mean, we've been climbing for –

Rockfist clicks the lighter. The stairs are lit again.

(*immediately*) Aaaahhhh! Hold on to me! Rockfist, hold on to me! Whatever you do, don't let go!

Rock What is it? What's the matter?

G

Kevin We've run out of stairs.

Rock You certain?

Kevin I'm certain. I've got one foot on nothing. Gently pull me back.

Rock OK.

Kevin Gently . . . gently!

Rock OK. I've got you. There.

Kevin regains his composure.

How deep is it there?

Kevin I don't know. We're very high up. Listen to the wind.

Rock You still reckon he's waiting for tomorrow to kill you.

Kevin No. Strange. We must have altered the sequence of events somehow.

Rock Right. Well, the next sequence of events is as follows. We're not sleeping here tonight. I don't know about you but I don't want to wake up dead. I am leading the way down these stairs and we are leaving this house right now. And I'll take my chance out on the moor. Because I'm not being locked up in here with a homicidal Scotchman. Now follow me.

Kevin I wonder what that knocking was?

Rock He's probably building a gallows, now come on.

They descend the stairs a lot faster than they climbed them.

Kevin (*as they go*) Not too fast.

Rock All right, we're on street level. Now let's get the heck out of here.

They move back through the kitchen, surprising Ebenezer as they do. He is counting money.

Ebenezer (*seeing them, alarmed*) Aaaah! Are ye alive? O man, are ye alive?

Kevin No thanks to you. You sent us up there deliberately.

Ebenezer It was a mistake, Davie, a mortal mistake. I never meant to kill ye. If I'd known . . . O, if I'd known . . . I would never have . . .

Kevin We're leaving now. You just be thankful we don't turn you over to the police.

Ebenezer Oh, no, you would not bring the law, Davie. You don't bring them for me, I will nae bring them for you.

Kevin For me? What do you mean, for me?

Ebenezer For stealing my gun. For stealing my blunderbuss.

Kevin We haven't stolen your gun. What are you talking about? (*to Rockfist*) He's saying we've stolen his gun now.

Ebenezer Well, if you didnae steal it, it must have been the other one.

Kevin What other one?

Ebenezer The lassie. The one who's just arrived. I let her in. She said she was your sister.

Kevin Sister? What sister are you talk –?

A loud bang. On the table, one or two things fly into the air.

Rock Get down!

The three crawl under the table.
Silence.
Monique's laugh is heard.

It's her.

Ebenezer Oh, my parritch. She's shot my parritch.

Rock Everybody OK?

Kevin Just about.

Rock Listen, if we move carefully we're probably OK. The thing about those kind of guns is that they're one-shot guns. They take a long time to re-load.

Kevin You certain about that?

Rock Kid, I may not know many things in life, but when it comes to guns, believe me, I'm an ex – (*He has brought his head up from under the table.*

Another big bang. He throws himself flat.) I guess
that may be a later model.

Kevin We can't stay under here. She'll pick us off
like –

Rock Like turkeys at Thanksgiving. I'll try bargain-
ing with her. (*calling*) Monique, listen. There's an
old Scotch guy under here. He's old and frail. He
ain't hurt nobody.

Kevin What?

Rock Poor old guy, he's bewildered and confused.
He's just lost his parritch. It's all he has in the
world, Monique. You let him come out, he'll be no
trouble, I promise. OK, Monique, he's coming out
now.

Kevin She'll kill him.

Rock I don't believe she can. Aren't we still in
Chapter Three?

Kevin As far as I know. I think so.

Rock And when does he die in the book, do you
know?

Kevin I don't think he does. Not in the book.

Rock So how can he die?

Kevin I suppose he can't.

Rock As far as the book's concerned, he's immortal.

Kevin Come to that, you never die in the books either.

Rock Correct, kid, I am also immortal. Until such time as my author decides to kill me off.

Kevin Then if he's immortal and you're immortal, then why –?

Rock Because you ain't, kid. You are very, very mortal. You're the one around here that can die, Kieron. And you're the one the lady is trying to kill. Sorry to break it to you.

Kevin (*digesting this*) Oh.

Rock Me, I just get locked in ovens.

Kevin Then why don't you just walk out there and take the gun off her.

Rock Because I don't know if you've ever been shot, Kinsey, but it damn well hurts. So we'll send the old guy out. Serve him right. Soon as he's out, make a break for the front door. (*to Ebenezer*) Hey, you!

Ebenezer Wha', wha'?

Rock (*shoving him*) Out! Go on out!

Ebenezer (*coming reluctantly out from under the table*) Nae, ye cannae . . . ye cannae . . .

Another loud bang. Ebenezer yells and rushes about the room.

Rock Come on!

Rockfist and Kevin make a dash for the front door.

(*as they do this*) Run, kid, keep running . . .

Further bangs as they go and yells from Ebenezer.
  Kevin and Rockfist leave the house.
  Sound of the wind again.

Ah! Fresh air!

Kevin Where are we going?

Rock As far away from there as possible . . .

They rush off. The lights change abruptly as we move to another book. It is a realm of bright primary colours.
  They enter immediately and stop, breathless.

This is better. A little bright perhaps, but better. I won't ask you where we are because I'm sure as usual you haven't the faintest idea.

Kevin I don't recognize this at all. I don't think this is even one of my books.

Rock You mean we have now wandered into somebody else's book? Who are we talking about? The guy next door?

Kevin I have a feeling this book belongs to Rachel . . .

Rock Rachel?

At this point, Baby Woobly comes skipping across.

B. Woobly (*singing to himself*) Woobly . . . woobly . . . woobly . . . woo . . . (*He goes off.*)

Rock What in the heck . . .?

Kevin Oh, no . . .

Rock What was *that*?

Kevin It's Baby Woobly.

Rock Baby who?

Kevin This is my sister's book. It's one of the Woobly books.

Rock (*with increasing agitation*) I do not believe this. I am a top-rated private investigator, fully licensed by the city of Los Angeles Justice Department. I have two public commendations and a special police medal. There are thirty-four books so far written to commemorate my successful fight against crime. I am translated into twenty-six languages and celebrated from South America to the continent of mainland Europe. In Argentina, I am known as *El Hombre* and in France, Europe, as *L'Homme Incroyable*. Now here I am in a Woobly book. How am I going to live this down? How am I going to face the police department again? How am I ever going to track down a serious criminal without him laughing in my face? What are you doing to me? Why are you doing this to me, Kelvin?

Kevin (*yelling*) Kevin!

Rock (*yelling*) Kevin!

Kevin Look, I'm sorry. There's no point in getting over-excited. My sister, Rachel, has obviously left this book on my bookshelf. She's always doing it. I've asked her not to but she keeps doing it. It's not my fault. She's very unreasonable.

Rock How old is she?

Kevin She's four.

Rock Yeah, well. I guess I was unreasonable at four.

Kevin You're unreasonable now. (*He sits angrily, apart from Rockfist.*)

Rock (*chastened*) Hey! Hey! Kid. So. Give me the lowdown. What gives with these Woobly books?

Kevin They're kids' books, that's all. The Wooblies. There's dozens of them. Rachel collects them. They're first readers with big pictures. All the words have got dashes in them.

Rock Details, kid, I need details. How many Wooblies are we dealing with here?

Kevin I don't know, I don't read them, do I?

Rock How many? I need to know what we're up against here.

76

Kevin Depends on which book. There's Baby Woobly.

Rock Baby Woobly. That's the one we just saw?

Kevin He's in all the books. And – Daddy Woobly. He's usually in most of them. And Mummy Woobly. And possibly Cousin Woobly. And Auntie Woobly, Uncle Woobly, Grandfather Woobly, Grandmother Woobly, Great-aunt Woobly . . .

Rock Hold it! Hold it! How dangerous are these things?

Kevin Oh, they're not dangerous. They just – jump about and sing and eat jelly, mostly.

Rock I don't wish to alarm you but we currently have – (*consulting his watch*) – twenty-three hours to go – it's jumped again. Time is running out, Kendal. There is little time left for jelly eating.

A disembodied voice suddenly speaks softly.

Voice It was hot. The sun was shin – ing.

Baby Woobly appears.

Hoo – ray! said Ba – by Woo – bly.

B. Woobly Woobly . . . woobly . . . woobly . . . !

Rock I think it's time to get out of here.

They move to go off in another direction.

Voice Can we go for a pic – nic, Dad – dy

Woo – bly, said Ba – by Woo – bly.

B. Woobly Woobly . . . woobly . . . woobly . . . ?

Daddy Woobly appears, blocking their escape.

Voice You must ask Mum – my Woo – bly, said
Dad – dy Woobly.

D. Woobly Woobly . . . woobly . . . woobly . . .

Rock (*leading off in another direction*) If he's a
vegetarian, I'll eat my socks. Come on, this way . . .

Voice Can we go for a pic – nic, Mum – my
Woo – bly, said Ba – by Woo – bly.

*Mummy Woobly appears, blocking their path.
They are surrounded now by Wooblies.*

B. Woobly Woobly . . . woobly . . . woobly . . .?

Rock We're surrounded. Take no prisoners.

Voice Yes, we can, said Mum – my Woo – bly.

M. Woobly Woobly . . . woobly . . . woobly . . .

Voice Hoo – ray, said Ba – by Woo – bly.

B. Woobly Woobly . . . woobly . . . woobly!

Rock Let 'em go on the picnic. With any luck they
won't notice us.

Voice May I ask my friends too, said Ba – by
Woo – bly.

B. Woobly Woobly . . . woobly . . . woobly?

Rock Oh – oh . . .

Kevin Don't speak too soon.

Voice Yes, you can, said Mum – my Woo – bly.

M. Woobly Woobly . . . woobly . . . woobly . . .

Voice Hoo – ray, said Ba – by Woo – bly.

B. Woobly Woobly . . . woobly . . . woobly . . .!

Voice And he went and asked his friends.

Baby Woobly goes to Kevin.

Ba – by Woo – bly went first to ask Wil – ly
Wiff – el.

Rock (*laughing*) Willy Wiffel!

B. Woobly Woobly . . . woobly . . . woobly . . . ?

Silence.

Voice Oh yes, please, Ba – by Woo – bly, said
Wil – ly Wiff – el.

Rock I think he's wanting an answer. You'd better
answer or he'll eat you.

Kevin (*hesitantly*) – er . . . Woobly. Woobly.
Woobly.

Voice Ba – by Woo – bly was so ex – ci – ted . . .!

B. Woobly Woobly . . . woobly . . . woobly . . .!

Voice Next he asked his friend Don – ny Din – gle.

Rock Who?

Kevin (*laughing*) Donny Dingle!

B. Woobly Woobly . . . woobly . . . woobly . . .?

Voice Oh yes, please, Ba – by Woo – bly, said Don – ny Din – gle.

Kevin Your turn.

Rock (*reluctantly*) Woobly. (*Pause.*) Woobly. (*Pause.*) Woobly.

Voice Ba – by Woo – bly was so ex – ci – ted . . .!

B. Woobly Woobly . . . woobly . . . woobly . . .!

Voice The Woo – blies were so hap – py that they danced and sang with their friends . . .

The Wooblies join hands with Kevin and Rockfist and dance in a ring.

Wooblies (*singing*)
Woobly, woobly, woobly woo . . .
Woobly, woobly, woo.
Woobly, woobly, woobly, woobly,
Woobly, woobly, wooooo!

They all fall down at the end with cries of delight.

Rock Kid, I don't think I can take much more of this.

Voice Mum – my and Dad – dy Woo – bly laid out the rug.

Mummy and Daddy Woobly lay out a large rug.

Ba – by Woo – bly was very exci – ted!

B. Woobly (*excitedly*) Woobly – woobly – woobly!

Voice So were Wil – ly Wiff – el and Don – ny Din – gle.

Kevin Woobly – woobly – woobly! (*to Rockfist*) Come on!

Rock No, I'm not doing any more.

Kevin What?

Rock I'm not doing any more woobling. I'm a grown man with bullet wounds. It's all right for you, kid, but I'm not jumping around, not for nobody.

The Wooblies have all stopped and are watching him.

(*to them all*) You hear me, you lot, you leave me out of it!

D. Woobly (*rather menacingly*) Woobly – woobly – woobly!

M. Woobly (*likewise*) Woobly – woobly – woobly!

B. Woobly (*likewise*) Woobly – woobly – woobly!

Kevin I think you've upset them.

Rock Too bad.

81

D. Woobly (*advancing on Rockfist*) Woobly – woobly – woobly!

M. Woobly (*likewise*) Woobly – woobly – woobly!

B. Woobly (*likewise*) Woobly – woobly – woobly!

Rock (*alarmed*) WOOBLY – WOOBLY – WOOBLY!

The Wooblies resume their tasks.

Voice When they had laid out the rug they all sat down.

They all sit down in a circle on the rug.

Dad – dy Woo – bly op – ened the pic – nic bask – et while Mum – my Woo – bly found the jel – ly bibs.

They proceed to do this, Mummy Woobly producing three large colourful bibs from her bag.

One for Ba – by Woo – bly!

Mummy Woobly ties a bib on Baby Woobly.

B. Woobly (*as she does this*) Woobly – woobly – woobly!

Voice One for Wil – ly Wiff – el!

Mummy Woobly ties a bib on Kevin.

Kevin (*as she does this*) Woobly – woobly – woobly!

Voice One for Don – ny Din – gle!

Mummy Woobly ties a bib on Rockfist.

Rock (*as she does this, nearly getting strangled*)
Woobly – woobly – warrggh!

Voice What has Dad – dy Woo – bly put in the
bask – et?

Kevin Jelly.

Voice Can you guess?

Kevin Jelly! (*to Rockfist*) It's always jelly.

Voice Can you guess what Dad – dy Woo – bly has
put in the bask – et?

Kevin I said, jelly!

Voice Have an – other guess!

Rock Jelly, for crying out loud! Now, get on with it!

Voice No. Have another guess.

Kevin Jelly. It has to be jelly.

Voice No. Have an – other guess. What is
bright – ly col – oured and goes wobb – le,
wobb – le, wobb – le . . .

Rock My sister-in-law . . .

Voice Can you guess?

Rock How many more times? J – E – L – E. Jel – ly.

Voice Right! Jel – ly!

Kevin Well done. Of course, we have to split the
words up.

Rock Hoo. Ray!

Voice The Woo – blies and their friends were so hap – py that they had to dance all ov – er a – gain.

The Wooblies spring to their feet bringing Rockfist and Kevin with them. They form the dancing, singing circle as before, all joining hands.

Kevin (*as they do so*) Here we go again!

Wooblies (*singing*)
Woobly, woobly, woobly woo . . .
Woobly, woobly, woo.
Woobly, woobly, woobly, woobly,
Woobly, woobly, wooooo!

They all fall down at the end with cries of delight.

Voice Dad – dy Woo – bly now serves out the jel – ly. A bowl for Ba – by Woo – bly!

Daddy Woobly fills a coloured bowl with jelly and hands it to Mummy Woobly, who serves Baby Woobly. She also gives him a large wooden spoon.

A bowl for Wil – ly Wiff – el.

Kevin is similarly served with jelly and given a spoon.

And a bowl for Don – ny Din – gle.

Rockfist is also served.

Rock (*consulting his watch*) Nineteen hours to go and I'm sitting here eating jello.

Voice Now, said Mum – my Woo – bly. Sit and eat your jel -ly nice – ly, chil – dren. Dad – dy Woo – bly and I are go – ing for a walk.

M. Woobly Woobly – woobly – woobly!

Mummy and Daddy Woobly go off, hand in hand. Baby Woobly eats his jelly.

Rock What kind of parents are those? Abandoning kids in a forest with bowls of jello.

Kevin This may be our chance to get away. I won-der where Monique is?

Rock I hope she's not around here. That woman starts up here, we could be knee deep in dead Wooblies . . .

Kevin We may have lost her back there. She may be still at the House of Shaws.

Rock Possibly. But knowing her, there's a nasty alternative.

Kevin What's that?

Rock That she's gone on ahead of us. She's there waiting for us in the next chapter.

Kevin You think so?

Rock It's possible.

Kevin Come on, we'd better go before they come

back. (*He gets to his feet.*)

Voice When Mum – my Woo – bly and Dad – dy Woo – bly had gone, Ba – by Woo – bly be – came very naught – y. He took some jel – ly in his spoon and threw it at Don – ny Din – gle.

B. Woobly (*throwing a spoonful of jelly at Rockfist*) Woobly – woobly – woobly!

Rock (*angrily*) Hey! Cut that out!

Voice How they all laughed! Ba – by Woo – bly did it again!

Baby Woobly throws another spoonful at Rockfist.

Rock You do that once more and I'll flatten you, buster.

Kevin Rockfist, leave him! Come on, quickly!

Voice Ba – by Woo – bly did it again.

Baby Woobly throws another spoonful at Rockfist.

Rock (*angrily*) Right! You asked for it buddy-boy.

Rockfist takes his own bowl and spoon and throws some jelly at Baby Woobly.

B. Woobly Woobly – woobly – woobly!

Rock Yeah! Woobly – woobly – woobly!

Baby Woobly throws some jelly at Rockfist again.

Rockfist throws some jelly at Baby Woobly.

Kevin (*trying to stop this*) What are you doing? We've no time for this.

Baby Woobly throws jelly at Rockfist. Rockfist ducks. Kevin gets it instead.

Rock (*triumphantly*) Ha! Ha! Woobly!

Kevin Oy! (*grabbing his own bowl and spoon*) Right!

A full-scale jelly fight breaks out between the three of them amidst lots of cries of 'Woobly!'
It culminates in Rockfist jamming the large serving bowl of jelly on Baby Woobly's head.

Rock Yeah!

Kevin Nice one!

Mummy and Daddy Woobly have returned during this, unseen by the others. Rockfist and Kevin notice them, belatedly.
A silence.

Voice When Mum – my and Dad – dy Woo – bly came back, oh dear! What a mess!

M. Woobly (*crossly*) Woobly – woobly – woobly!

D. Woobly (*crossly*) Woobly – woobly – woobly!

Rock I guess we're in trouble.

Voice Mum – my and Dad – dy Woo – bly be – gan to clear up the mess.

Mummy Woobly folds up the rug whilst Daddy Woobly packs away the bowls and spoons in the basket.

They pre – ten – ded to be ve – ry cross in – deed.

M. Woobly (*crossly*) Woobly – woobly – woobly!

D. Woobly (*crossly*) Woobly – woobly – woobly!

Voice You've been such bad chil – dren you don't de – serve an – y sup – per, said Mum – my Woo – bly.

M. Woobly Woobly – woobly – woobly!

Voice We're go – ing home now and you can all three get in – to a good hot bath.

Rock Oh, no . . . That's it! There's no way I'm tak-ing a bath with a Woobly! Run for it!

A chase.
  Lots more cries of 'Woobly!'
  Finally, Mummy and Daddy Woobly capture the others. Daddy Woobly holds Baby Woobly's and Kevin's hands. Mummy Woobly has hold of Rockfist's hand.

Hell! This thing's got a grip like a grizzly bear.

Kevin Quickly! Take my hand!

Rock What?

Kevin I've got an idea.

Rockfist grabs hold of Kevin's hand.

Now, can you grab Baby Woobly's hand?

Rock I hope you know what you're doing . . .

*He grabs Baby Woobly's hand. They are now
nearly standing in a circle.*

Kevin (*starting off the singing*)
Woobly, woobly, woobly woo . . .

*Baby Woobly immediately grabs Mummy
Woobly's spare hand so that they've formed a
circle again.*

Wooblies (*joining in*)
Woobly, woobly, woo.
Woobly, woobly, woobly, woobly,
Woobly, woobly, wooooo!

Kevin And again! (*singing*)
Woobly, woobly, woo . . .

*As they start to sing again, Kevin and Rockfist
slip out of the circle and join up Mummy and
Daddy Woobly's hands.*

Wooblies (*joining in again*)
Woobly, woobly, woo.
Woobly, woobly, woobly, woobly,
Woobly, woobly, wooooo!

*Rockfist and Kevin have run off. The Wooblies,
having finished their song, collapse on the
ground as before.*
    *They sit up and realize that the other two
have gone.*

89

D. Woobly (*puzzled*) Woobly – woobly – woobly!

M. Woobly (*very puzzled*) Woobly – woobly – woobly!

B. Woobly (*completely baffled*) Woobly – woobly – woobly!

Voice And the Woo – blies sad – ly ga – thered up all their things . . .

The Wooblies do this.

Where have Wil – ly Wiff – el and Don – ny Din – gle gone, asked Ba – by Woo – bly.

B. Woobly Woobly – woobly – woobly?

Voice They have gone in – to the deep, dark wood, said Mum – my Woo – bly sad – ly.

M. Woobly (*sadly*) Woobly – woobly – woobly . . .

Voice We shall never see them again, said Dad – dy Woob – ly.

D. Woobly Woobly – woobly – woobly . . .

Voice For no – bo – dy re – turns from the deep, dark wood.

A distant clap of thunder.

And the Woo – blies hur – ried home for it was start – ing to rain.

D. Woobly Woobly – woobly – woobly!

M. Woobly Woobly – woobly – woobly!

B. Woobly Woobly – woobly – woobly!

The Wooblies hurry off, taking their belongings with them.
   As they go, another clap of thunder, much louder. The scene changes. We are now in the traditional old dark house. Lightning flashes through the windows as Rockfist and Kevin re-enter.

Rock Another book?

Kevin Must be.

Rock Any idea what?

Kevin Yes. I think I do.

Rock OK. Break it to me gently. Where are we now? Frankenstein's castle? Edgar Allen Poe land. The Addams Family Home?

Another thunderclap.

The Boys' Book of Weather Forecasts?

Kevin I don't like to tell you.

Rock Come on! Out with it!

Kevin I think it's my book of ghost stories!

Another really loud thunderclap. They are both momentarily startled, cry out and grab hold of each other.

Kevin and Rock Wah!

Rock (*immediately recovering*) All right! All right! All right! Calm down! Keep calm! You got to remember just one thing, kid. There's no such things as ghosts, OK? They're all in your mind. They can only get in there, inside your head, if you let 'em, right?

Kevin Yes.

Rock Look at it this way. I've been around for years and years and I never met a ghost yet, OK?

Kevin OK.

Rock Remember. There's no such things.

A loud creak from somewhere.

(*jumping*) WHAT WAS THAT!!!!!?

Kevin It's all right! It was just a creak.

Rock All right! Well, don't start jumping about! That's the way to panic. Keep calm, OK?

Kevin You know, I'm not sure. I think, possibly, this might be the last book.

Rock It is?

Kevin Possibly. I think this could lead back to my bedroom. I'm not a hundred per cent sure.

Rock Then we'd better start looking for your bedroom. The sooner the better. There's about a thousand doors in this place.

Kevin Then let's start upst –

Rock Ssshhh!

Kevin What?

Rock You hear that?

Kevin What?

Rock There's somebody moving about upstairs.

Kevin I don't hear anything.

Rock Sssshh!

They listen. No sound.

I thought I heard something. Come on.

They move forward cautiously.
A clatter from above.
They freeze.

There it is. Somebody's up there.

Kevin Or something.

Rock No. Some*one*. Not some*thing*. Some*one*.
There's no such thing as a something. The only
thing the something can be is a someone. OK?

Kevin OK.

Another clatter from somewhere.

Rock (*jumping*) WHAT WAS THAT!!!!!?

Kevin Shhh!

Rock I hope my gun works in this place. We may
need it. Follow me upstairs.

They climb the stairs cautiously, pausing now and again.
Occasional thunder and lightning.

See anything?

Kevin Nothing.

Rock We'd better try a few of these doors.

He steps forward to try a door knob. The sound of a door creaking open.

I don't want to worry you, but the door opened on its own.

They hesitate.

You want to take a look inside?

Kevin After you.

Rock (*reluctantly*) OK. (*He hesitates.*) You know, I think you should be the one to take a look inside first. I mean, this could be your bedroom, you see. And I wouldn't recognize your bedroom if I saw it, whereas you would recognize your bedroom if you saw it. So it makes more sense for you to go in first and identify it as your bedroom, that's all I'm saying.

Kevin doesn't move.

You want me to go in first?

Kevin Yes.

Rock OK.

*He moves cautiously through the doorway.
Sudden fierce dog barking causes him to jump
back with a cry.*

Aaaaahhhh! It was a dog! A dog! Did you see the
dog?

Kevin No.

Rock It was there. A giant dog. With great big
teeth.

Kevin That's the phantom hound of Caroon.

Rock The what?

Kevin (*dramatically*) When his evil master,
Edmund Earl of Caroon, died his dog returned to
guard the doorway of his master's bedchamber.
According to the curse of the Caroons no one may
enter, nor may Edmund's tormented spirit leave
until he has atoned for his terrible sins during his
lifetime. And on certain nights you can see him
walking –

Rock All right, all right. Knock it off. This ain't
your bedroom, OK. That's all we need to know.
This book you did read, I take it?

Kevin Oh, yes. Lots of times.

Rock So what else have we got in store?

Kevin Well, there's the Headless Monk –

Rock Great . . .

Kevin The woman with the bloodstained hands . . .

Rock Tremendous.

Kevin The weird child who floats on the ceiling . . .

Rock Wonderful.

Kevin The killer cat . . .

Rock OK. That'll do. Don't tell me any more, it'll spoil the surprise. Next room. Follow me.

They move on.

When we get to your room, the first thing you do is find the book. My book. You turn to the end and discover the true identity of the Green Shark. According to my watch we're down to four hours, kid. Time's jumped forward again. We got no time to lose. (*He pushes another door, which creaks open.*) Wait there. I can't afford to lose you.

He goes off into the next room. Kevin waits rather nervously.

Kevin (*singing to himself*)
Woobly, woobly, woobly woo . . .
Woobly, woobly, woo.
Woobly, woobly, woobly, woobly –

Thunder and lightning come together. For a second, a ghostly figure is silhouetted in the passageway behind him.

(*calling*) Rockfist!

Rockfist rushes out of the bedroom.

Rock What is it?

Kevin There was somebody back there.

Rock You sure?

Kevin I saw them. I couldn't see who it was. Just a figure.

Rock Monique?

Kevin Maybe.

Rock It figures. She did, she cut ahead of us. We'd better keep moving. Here! (*He hands Kevin his lighter.*) Take my lighter. Don't waste fuel but if you think you see anything again, just click it and take a closer look. You may even frighten it away.

Kevin Right.

Rock Follow on. Keep your eyes open.

Kevin (*miserably*) We'll never find my room . . .

Rock Don't give up, kid. We've come this far, haven't we? Through chessmen and Red Riding Hood and mad Scotchmen and Wooblies – we're not going to give up now. Any time around the next bend we could come across your – aaaaaahhhh! (*He suddenly vanishes. He appears to have fallen down a deep well.*)

Kevin Rockfist!

Silence. Kevin goes to the edge of the well and

looks down it cautiously.

(*calling, echoing*) Rockfist!

   A groan from below.

Are you all right? Rockfist?

Rock (*echoing from the well*) What happened?

Kevin You seem to have fallen down – it seems to be a well.

Rock Yep. It feels like a well.

   Sound of exertion.

Kevin Can you climb out?

Rock (*with more exertion*) Wait a – Hurrp! Just a – Hurrp! Hurrp! No. Too slippery.

Kevin Just a second. I'll try and find a sheet or something . . .

Rock (*from the well*) Watch out, kid. That's all. Monique's around here somewhere, I know it.

   Kevin starts to move off.

Kevin I'll be as quick as I can. There must be a sheet in one of these – Aaah!

   He comes (metaphorically) face to face with the Headless Monk. Its head, as is traditional, is under its arm.

Oh, help!

Monk (*in a ghastly voice*) Beware!

Rock What's happening up there?

Kevin It's the monk! I'll be back!

Rock Don't leave me down here, kid!

The Monk advances on Kevin.

Kevin Sorry, Rockfist. I'll be back when I can.

He rushes off, with the Monk following.

Rock Hey! Come back! Don't leave me down here, kid. We got two hours now. That's all we've got! Come back!

Kevin races back on. He pulls up short. We are back in his bedroom.

Kevin (*looking around him, incredulously*) I don't believe it. It's my room! I'm home. I'm home! (*looking around*) Now. The book. I just need the book. *Rockfist Slim and the Case of the Green Shark.*

He takes the book and starts rapidly leafing through the pages.
   Monique appears in the doorway.

Monique Hallo, Kevin.

Kevin (*freezing*) Monique! (*He hastily conceals the book.*)

Monique Welcome home, Kevin.

Kevin How did you –? How did you get here?

Monique Just like you, *chéri*, I followed – how you say – my nose. But unlike you and the absurd Rockfist, I did not waste time on stupid diversions.

Kevin What are you doing here? What do you want?

Monique We have a little score to settle, Kevin, don't we, *mon ami*? Little boys who bite must be taught lessons.

Kevin You come near me, I'll yell the place down. I warn you! My dad's next door.

Monique Please! Sssshhh! No noise. We would not want to wake your sister, would we, Kevin? I have just been in to see her. She is sleeping so peaceful.

Kevin You leave Rachel alone. I'm warning you . . .

Monique Where's the book, Kevin?

Kevin What book?

Monique Come, the book.

Kevin I don't know what you're talking about?

Monique Very well. Maybe I shall wake Rachel to see if she knows where is the book.

Kevin hesitates.

You would prefer that?

Kevin (*reluctantly producing the book*) Here. Here you are, take it then.

Monique *Non*. You still have the lighter? Come along, Rockfist's lighter. You have it. I know you have it, Kevin, I have been watching. Come.

Kevin What if I do?

Monique Because I want you to take that book and burn it, Kevin.

Kevin Burn it?

Monique I want you to destroy it for me. Now.

Kevin I can't do that.

Monique Then I will fetch Rachel.

Kevin Look, if I destroy the book, won't it – won't it destroy everything in it? Won't it destroy Rockfist?

Monique Of course.

Kevin I can't do that. He's a friend, he's –

Monique makes a move to the door.

Wait! Just a minute. If I burn this book, won't I destroy you as well? I'll destroy you, I'll destroy the Green Shark, I'll destroy everyone.

Monique Perhaps.

Kevin Well, what would be the point of that?

Monique Kevin, if you finish the book, you will

find that I, Monique, die anyway.

Kevin You do? Good.

Monique Killed, of course, by the indestructible Rockfist. How do you think it feels, Kevin, always to die? Always by the hand of this same absurd stupid little man in his silly hat. How do you think it feels to be this superior being, *moi*, brought down by this gum-chewing little troll? This time, Kevin, if I die, as I will surely die, this time he will also die. *Vive la criminalité, en bas les Américains, vive la France.*

Kevin So it was Rockfist you were after all the time.

Monique Of course.

Kevin He thought you were after me.

Monique You? You are nothing. You are but a prawn in the game.

Kevin Pawn.

Monique Now burn the book, please. Before someone else gets burnt.

Kevin (*throwing the book and the lighter on to the bed*) You want him dead, you kill him.

Monique No. You must do it. Do it!

Kevin Why don't you?

Monique You, Kevin. I command.

102

Kevin No, you!

Monique hesitates.

You can't, can you? You can't burn it, can you? You can't even pick up the lighter. Because – wait a minute – you can't touch anything here, can you? Not in this room, this world. Not in my world. Because you don't belong here. You belong in a book, don't you? Not in the real world. In the real world, you can't hurt me at all. You can't hurt anyone.

Monique Kevin . . .

Kevin Go away! Get out of my room! Get out of this house!

Monique I warn you, Kevin, I will –

Kevin Don't threaten me! You can't do anything. Nothing. Now get out.

Monique (*as she goes*) Keviiinnnn!

Kevin Get out!

Monique Kevvviiiiinnnnnnnnnn!

She has gone. Kevin is alone once more. He takes up the book. He stands uncertainly.

Kevin Rockfist . . . What am I going to do? (*He thumbs through the end of the book.*) The Green Shark? The Green Shark? Where is it? (*finding it and reading briefly*) Oh, no! Of course! Of course! (*He throws the Rockfist book on to the bed.*) Now, how do I –? I know! Yes. (*He takes* The Book of Ghost Stories *from the shelf. As an afterthought, he also pulls the top sheet off his bed.*) Sorry, Mum. (*reading*) 'The headless monk glided through the corridors . . .' Come on! 'The spectre glided towards him, a terrible expression of deep sorrow on the face that was tucked under the monk's arm.' Why isn't it working? It ought to work . . .

The room is growing darker.

'The onlookers remained rooted to the spot. The monk turned one last time and surveyed them. He seemed deep in thought, as if in possession of some dread knowledge, as though pondering some dire warning. At last he seemed to come to a conclusion. Casting its fearful eyes upon them it uttered one single word:'

We are now back in the darkness of the haunted house.
The Headless Monk has reappeared.

Monk Beware! (*He glides away.*)

Kevin Done it! (*calling*) Rockfist! Rockfist!

Rockfist's voice is heard from the well, as before.

Rock Hey, kid! Where you been?

Kevin Oh, thank heavens! I thought perhaps you might have drowned.

Rock Yes, well, what's that to you? Yes, I could have drowned easy. Except there's no water down here, I could be dead, kid.

Kevin starts to lower the sheet down the well.

Kevin Here! Take the end of this. All right?

Rock All right! Brace yourself, I'm coming up.

Kevin sits grasping the sheet and taking the strain.
 Rockfist starts climbing out. Effortful noises.

Can you hold it?

Kevin Yes, yes. Just be quick.

Rock I'm being as quick as I can. (*as he climbs*) Have you – seen – Monique?

Kevin Yes. She was waiting for me in my room.

Rock She was?

Kevin It wasn't me she was after, it was you.

Rock That a fact?

Kevin She thought by burning the book, she could destroy you.

Rock (*as he reaches the top*) Poor dame. Not a chance. She didn't stand a chance.

Kevin No?

Rock Even if she'd burnt the book . . .

Kevin Why not?

They are both sitting on the floor, recovering from their exertions.

Rock I gave her credit for more brains. Kid, do you know how many books I'm in? If she wanted to get at me, she'd have to burn every copy of thirty-four different books all over the world in over twenty-six languages. I told you, kid, I'm immortal. They can't touch me. You see, with a book, it's immortal. It's in your head. It lives for ever. Now, come on, first things first. Did you find out the identity of the Green Shark?

Kevin I did.

Rock Well, come on. Let's have it. I have less than – (*consulting his watch*) – twenty-nine minutes to save the world.

Kevin (*smiling*) I just don't want to spoil the end of the book for you.

Rock Hey, come on – stop kidding around here –

Kevin OK. Well, all right. The Green Shark is Monique herself.

Rock (*blankly*) Monique.

Kevin When you think about it, it had to be. She was the only one close to him – she gave out all his orders. She was the only person who apparently ever talked to him or even saw him.

Rock Of course, of course it had to be Monique. I suspected that all along. I'd have got there, don't worry. Listen, I got to go. Clear up the case. You know your way home from here?

Kevin Yes.

Rock (*taking Kevin's hand*) It's been a pleasure to work with you. I tell you, if I was the kind of guy who needed a partner, you'd be the one. But I need a partner like a hole in the top of my head, so forget it.

Kevin It's been great. Good luck.

Rock You bet!

Kevin If there's ever anything I can do . . .

Rock Hey! Just keep reading the books. That's what keeps us people going. So long – Kevin.

Kevin So long – Rockfist.

Rock It's time you called me Rock. R – O – C – K. Spelt indestructible.

He goes. Kevin is alone.

Kevin (*faintly*) Goodbye.

The lights change and he is back in his bedroom. He goes to the bookcase and replaces The Book of Ghost Stories. *He also tidies away the Rockfist book. He gets into bed.*

Dad (*off*) Kevin! Is that light of yours still on?

Kevin I only put it on for a second, Dad.

Dad Well, turn it off. I won't tell you again. All this reading. It's not good for you. You'll just give yourself dreams. You don't want to have dreams, do you, son?

Kevin Oh, no, Dad. That would never do. (*He switches off his light. Softly*) Good night, Rockfist. See you tomorrow.

Blackout.